Fracture LINES

GRACE YOUNG

iUniverse LLC
Bloomington

FRACTURE LINES

iUniverse books may be ordered through booksellers or by contacting:

iUniverse LLC
1663 Liberty Drive
Bloomington, IN 47403
www.iuniverse.com
1-800-Authors (1-800-288-4677)

ISBN: 978-1-4917-3028-7 (sc)
ISBN: 978-1-4917-3030-0 (hc)
ISBN: 978-1-4917-3029-4 (e)

Library of Congress Control Number: 2014905703

Printed in the United States of America.

iUniverse rev. date: 5/15/2014

Dedication

To my dear Lord who gave me the strength to write this book

My Mother whose limited times here on earth
blessed everyone she met.

Acknowledgements

To my dear friends, and you know who you are.
Anne, Rae
Steve, Tom

My son, daughter, and granddaugter
And counselors who taught me it was never about me

Preface

This cathartic, inspirational book was written to empower many women whose voices have been silenced. It was also written for the men who love them. Some may call this shattered silence, but I simply cannot ruminate about what is wrong or right anymore. For me, the time is now.

We must grasp each other's hands and tell our stories loudly, saying good-bye to the nightmares that haunt us day and night and to the voices that say we are not good enough, those that defeat who we were meant to be. Now is the time to let our lights shine and show our brilliance. None of us can control what happened to us when we had no voice or were too young to know we had a voice, and certainly this was never ever about us. The actions of others never define us, but we take them along with us in life, believing somehow we were at fault, leading us into a maze of despair.

Are you starting to recognize yourself here? Do you remember those dark times when you had no voice, no empowerment? What have you taken into your life from this, and how has it affected you? We all are wounded warriors, and the scars are there. These scars manifest themselves by oozing through our personalities, social skills, addictions, relationships, parenting, and family ties. As for me, these scars have become fracture lines. A fracture may heal, but I personally will probably never forget exactly where that fracture occurred and what caused it.

Writing this has not been easy. I speak to people daily, and I speak from my heart and soul. The memories are always present for me. Time does not make it any easier.

Like others, I've learned to mask my memories and use diversions so life is bearable. The time is here and now to know that we are not alone. We are survivors, and we have fought and battled, which makes us warriors. We have the voice of empowerment, which is what this book is about. We can and will stand up for ourselves and others we know. It takes a very strong person to reach out to women who perhaps seem shy, reclusive, and aloof. A hug, smile, or caring gesture may be all they need to make the start into their journey of healing their anguish. We all need a shoulder to lean on, and sometimes family members are not available or are at the root of the problem.

My greatest wish if you are healing is that something you read in this book resonates with you, on any level, and you think to yourself, *Wow, finally, someone not only had the guts to write about this, but also has addressed how we can start empowerment groups all around the country!* We have a voice and it must be heard! Collectively there is no education level required either. Many victims turn into workaholics so they don't have to think about those years, those moments, those hurts, etc. Some do take on more powerful positions (e.g., doctors, attorneys, and such).

However, the vast majority shut down. Women need to help other women find their mojo, so to speak. If not now, when? Has there ever been a better time to talk about these taboo subjects that have been swept under the rug for years and are still eating us alive?

We listen to the talk shows, and yes, we read the books, but this book is about women starting empowerment circles all over the country, reclaiming their voices that they thought were lost. I know, from the bottom of my heart, we can sit in groups and say, "This was never your fault!" How great would that be? We can reclaim our lives at any age. It would be very empowering to hear those morose, deafening stories and free ourselves from those agonizing scars and fractures that have torn apart our minds and bodies—knowing someone cares!

So, as hard as it was to write my story—with many tears—I know there are worse stories out there. Let's start the movement. Let's hit this hard, and hopefully history will remember this as a time where we moved forward from anger, fear, and stress to hold our heads up and say, "It was never about me, and I am a survivor!"

There is a section at the end of this book for notes; please take notes and share in groups. I love each and every one of you! We are all miracles; remember this as you write your journal, share your story, and dig deep to take down those walls and heal those scars and fractures.

Let's all make our voices heard and let our bodies recover from stress-filled diseases. Let peace and grace fill your hearts, and let joy and laughter come back into your lives, no matter what has happened. We are all standing together, holding hands and hearts united.

Introduction

Most people seek closure to problems or issues in their lives. However, when problems are larger than life, how would one know if they would ever have the clarity of mind, patience, or peace to weather repeated storms again and again.

Fortitude is a word I am so familiar with. I just seek strength, peace of mind, believe in the best of others, and pray, pray, pray. My heart has been an open book, and I have worn out the sleeves of shirts with pounding gracious love. Honesty abounds, and I have had the life choked out of me by something akin to ivy growing abundantly out of control. There has been no rhyme or reason for the fractures in my life, only that they have occurred, and I am still here to write this book and, by doing so, help others. After an extended time of trying to steer my own wheel, God has taken over and given me a glimpse of what is to come.

We all dream of some realm of normalcy in our lives, yet the few who have it may not even recognize the splendor of it. Still, I continue to not only talk the talk, but also reverently walk the walk.

I'm all too familiar with the contradictory adage that whatever does not kill you makes you stronger. However, I still cannot comprehend that God gives so many hardships to the great of heart, and so much good to the impure of soul. Having said that, I do not believe God has anything to do with this statement at all. God is not an evil God, but he does know our heart and soul. Our minds are just so minuscule that we cannot possibly comprehend the greatness of what is coming, so we must count everything a lesson and a blessing.

As the rain pounds the dry soil of Florida, the place from which I embarked on my journey of finding myself and a reason for still being alive, my pen begins to move and my thoughts pour out faster than the rain. Perhaps this is the motivation needed to dredge out all the evildoers and tribulations I have been through. Perhaps this is what I need to help women from all over the world find their voices and empower them to speak up about their trials and tribulations.

Only when we are free from monsters and demons that battle us daily and command and domineer us—telling us we are not worthy of a voice—can we be completely free to love ourselves and one another. Only now am I realizing we have choices! Many of us have never been given choices, a blessed word.

I have been awestruck that this is the place where my mother was given her voice and where she was born. Never would I have thought I would return to find my heart, my answers, and the beginning of my journey. I hope to honor her courageous voice for all women as well as the men who love them and who have been through fractures of overwhelming proportions. Let this book be for all who have ever loved a woman who feels she cannot see through see past her walls or heal the fracture lines.

No one wants to live a broken life, have her voice taken away, live in torment, or be given no choices, and this is a story of my overwhelming fractures. Many women will have more and some less, and every story is significant. Each fracture is significant for each person, young or old. Most women I know deal with these by masking them and living in lonely misery. Many lead a life filled with addiction because it is much easier to be numb than face reality. Many will bury themselves in work and go on and on about how busy they are because that is their reality. And let's not forget that dark shadow that hangs over all of us, dragging and weighing us down.

We all live with voices in our minds—yes, those terrible voices. For the readers of this book, you will know what they are. Close your eyes and start to think of your first fracture. Was it in your younger years when your mother or father told you something that hit you like a ton of bricks, or was it in school when you felt like a horrific failure? Was it something much deeper, such as a death of a loved one? Were you raped? Did you fall into drugs and alcohol? Did something happen that was out of your control, and how did you respond?

There are numerous events in life that can take over our minds and shift our subconscious thoughts into controlled thought patterns. When this becomes repetitious, we start to believe and obsess about how we are different. We tend to become people pleasers, even when we know what we are doing is wrong. Shifting thought patterns emerge, and some women tend to isolate; some will draw attention to themselves by doing uncanny things, right down to hurting themselves; and others wish they would just die.

Many of us have our share of dysfunctional families. Some women never know the love of a mother. Some of us are mothers that perhaps never should have been. Others have been mothers that have given everything to their children because they had so little, and they never want their children to grow up like they had to.

Stress plays a huge role for fractured women. By not mending the tears as soon as possible, or by preventing the glue from setting, the mind plays havoc. And generally having a healthy relationship with anyone is very hard, if not impossible, to do. Many autoimmune diseases are thought to have been brought on by stress, which, in my opinion, has an underlying cause. Fractures of the heart and soul in an already tenuous woman will not allow a healthy relationship under any circumstance. These tend to be codependent or abusive relationships. Deep depression tends to settle in the mind, heart and bones to the point where daily functioning is unhealthy. True to form, women seek what they missed from a mother or father in their partners because they cannot love themselves first, which is an essential component.

How many breaks can you relate to? There are notes in the back of this book. Take them to study groups and seriously open up to one another or with your partner if you want a healthy loving relationship. Identify the fractures as far back as you can remember. Even if they seem small compared to what you are reading in *Fracture Lines*, they may be big to you. If they seem larger, write them down too.

We all need to talk, as we are not doing enough talking in this tech-savvy world. Families are not family units anymore and are divided through work or attitudes of "what can you do for me?" Greed has overcome God, which is horrific. Write to me, and tell me your thoughts. Help me carry out my work to make this world a better place for all to live. We are empowered women whose lights need to shine and whose stories need to be heard. We must never be silent about atrocities that still exist.

Help me to help you love. The journey of closure for all starts with baby steps, but that first step is amazing.

Fracture One

My Childhood

There is no heartbeat, Ann. She is blue.

This was relayed to me by my mother years later. Having lost a child a few years before me, my mother was very scared, but then the breath of life took hold with me. My mother wanted me to retain the name of the baby she had lost if I were to be a girl. That baby would have been born around Christmas but passed on before me.

I was born in a hospital in a small town in New York and, not long after, was whisked away to an even smaller town. There, my life as I now know it began. This tiny little town was one where everyone knew each other; it was supposed to be very safe for raising a family.

My mother had led somewhat a life of glamour, being raised in a family of class and money in Florida. But she was raised by nannies. Her mother and father were off traveling most of the time. I can only assume from what she told me that most of what she learned about love came from one very special nanny.

Her parents picked a summer home away from the heat of the South, and the only prerequisite was rail service into New York City. This small town provided a safe harbor for my mother as she raised her three girls. She also had relatives there who would come into play in many ways as well.

She was put into an all-girls boarding school, which she ran away from many times, and met a farm boy at the county fair. (Wow, sounds similar to *The Notebook* but with a very different ending.) Her father, my grandfather, was infuriated and told her, in no uncertain terms, if she married this man, this farmer, he would disown not only her, but also any children she would have. This is exactly what happened. Here, in this tiny little town with one traffic light, was the place where my mother settled down to raise three pretty, courageous girls.

Mom was the life of this small country town and was adored, as I adored her. She was a beautiful brunette with just a hint of a weight problem. However, as much love as she poured out, my father did his best to take it away by terrorizing us three girls and her. He was a farmer and worked long hours, and he would fly into alcoholic, abusive rages.

My mother just tried to sweep it under the rug for the sake of her girls. I often caught her crying, which just tugged at my heart and soul. How she could endure his indignant wrath was beyond my tiny scope of mind. She sewed most of our school clothes, all the drapes, and was always doing anything she could to save money.

Being the middle of three girls was hard and trying. I spent time at my cousin's house playing and watching TV. I was very inventive as well. In those days, you had to use your imagination. I would rake leaf houses and play with my turtles; I just loved animals.

My older sister, Sheryl, a very tall brunette who looked nothing like her two younger sisters was book smart but always challenging authority. Clearly she sought the love of my father, but she could never do anything right by him. Sheryl marched to the beat of a different drummer. Woodstock and the days of drugs and such would end up being her demise. No matter how book smart she was, common sense was not her forte.

In looking back, I see the toll our abusive, alcoholic father took in her life. My mother was always playing the role of the go-between, which was severely stressful. The attention she sought from my Dad, no matter what she did—or, for that matter, any of us did—was never going to be enough. He was always working at the farm, and then drinking. Mom made spectacular dinners, some of which dad never made due to his indulgence at the bars. I can still remember the sadness in her eyes when she had to put the dinner into the refrigerator.

Sheryl ended up ill with hepatitis later on. She really had no boyfriends and sought the wrong kind of attention from men. She was tall, skinny, and picked fights with just about everyone. However, I still thought she was beautiful and loved her just because she was my big sister. Throughout all of this, I could just never imagine why she said what she did to provoke my father, to the point of beatings and wrath, until she was finally kicked out when she had hepatitis.

When the arguing would become intolerable and I couldn't find a place to hide, I would imagine I could shrink myself to fit into a tiny doorway at the top of the steps. Inside was a beautiful kitchen and living-room area. There was no "noise." As I would enter another doorway, there was a full-size Olympic swimming pool, which was heated, and soft music was playing. This was the room I loved the most. For me, it was surreal and created a space where I felt transported out of time. This was my perfect hideaway, and no one knew about it but me. Over the course of many years, I went there many, many times.

When I told a counselor about this, she said I must have thought I was running away from something. I thought, *Well, if you only knew. Of course I was running away!* My friends did not live in houses like this. They, for the most part, had loving, if strict, parents. Comprehending extreme alcoholism and abuse at a very young age, with an enabling mother under extreme stress who would soon die, was not in my sense of reasoning and never should have been.

My younger sister, Joyce, was the polar opposite of Sheryl, although almost eight years separated them. She was more on the shy side. We were both a lot smaller in bone structure, and we were both blondes. However, Joyce seemed to get all the attention, as she never seemed to get in the middle of anyone or anything. I knew there was a lot of tension and pent up anger going on inside of her though. Sometimes, when I would talk to her, she would "mirror my words." In other words, if I said, "You are not going to the barn today," she would repeat those same words but without a voice to them. Yes, I am ashamed to say I picked on her unmercifully for this because I thought she was sassing me back. Now I know it had to do with a multitude of things, including stress.

Life for me in those early years was about bike rides and playing with cousins and friends. We were always inventing some new way to play. Those were the days when kids could leave in the morning and not come home until dinner. For some really special treats, we could go to my cousin's lake house and even water ski. There I was twice pulled from the water after nearly drowning

Once I was in a bassinet, and I tipped over into Moose Lake. My mother didn't know; I fell behind her. She had been talking with other women, and somehow the bassinet, with me in it, went right over and sunk. She would retell that story many times.

The other time, I was in the same lake playing when I could not swim well at the age of five. All the adults had left, and I was trying to swim to the Shore in shallow water. All I remember is ending up where the light choppy waves had washed me in. I clearly remember breathing underwater and wondering why no one was around. A peaceful feeling was all I could describe; this was strangely comforting.

My older cousin finally found and yanked me out of the water, yelling, "I found her!" Everyone crowded around my waterlogged, blue body. "What were you doing down here alone?"

I said, "Breathing underwater."

My eldest cousin said he witnessed this as well, but this was dismissed as crazy. I looked around and remembered feeling I wanted to go back to feeling safe, warm, and loved. Then I was wrapped up with towels and admonished to never go down to the dock again by myself. The lake was just never the same again to me.

Once a year, my mother would drive us to visit my grandmother in Florida for the whole month of January. Like normal kids, we did our best to make the trip a living hell. How she did this I will never know. We would visit with our cousins, aunt, uncle, and other relatives. The sun and warmth of Florida was so wonderful. I loved to fish (catch and release), and getting away from my father seemed to be just what the doctor had ordered. These trips felt like the best days of my life, and aside from the typical sibling and cousin bickering, they were.

We grew up in a very small, simple town, in a great neighborhood, where everyone knew each other's business. My first ten years were spent mostly riding my bike, making leaf houses, playing with my cousin and friends and, of course, playing on the swing set! What a great time for using one's imagination. I remember leaving the house early in the morning and not returning home until very late in the afternoon. No one seemed to care where we were; there was just an assumption that, at some point in time, we would be back when we got hungry.

Everyone loved my mom, and though her riches were gone, it was her humility and love for common folk that endeared her to everyone in this small town. She could whip up any recipe, sew our school clothes, drapes, and slip covers, and play the piano naturally. She had a natural golf swing. The only simple issue about her outside appearance was her weight. However, even at the age of eight or ten years of age, I knew she had much more of a problem than weight: My father.

One day, stepping into church, my mother paused and gazed into the sun in the sky. The sun was so strong, and its rays were streaking playfully across her brunette hair. I looked at her and thought, *She is so beautiful, but something is so wrong.* I knew my mother was not happy and very troubled about something. When I asked she would just say, "Nothing honey," or "Don't be silly."

In hindsight, I don't believe she passed one of her amazing traits on to me, although one of the remaining ladies she played golf with said, "She gave you her best trait—her personality." Little did she know I would hold this great statement dear to my heart forever.

I overheard her talking to a few select friends, who begged her to get out of the marriage. Surely she suffered from the "it will get better" syndrome. Then there was her father, who told her sternly never to marry him in the first place. How could she go to him and say he was right when he had nothing to do with her or his grandchildren in the first place? Her father by then had divorced and was married to his much younger secretary, thereby leaving my grandmother alone. How unscrupulous could he be? Damning my mother for marrying a classless farmer, but in essence defacing himself? One thing I did know for sure is that my mother did love her children and would have would have done anything for them. She went from a life of luxury to a life to a life of hell.

One day I recall my mother wanted to go with her friends to a hunting camp. I begged to go, as I had heard about a beautiful place in the woods with a stream. After all, at that moment I was thirteen years old and really starting to feel like an adult. We all walked about a mile into the woods, heading down a winding path, on a beautiful sunny day. We came across a path with brilliant sunshine spreading through the trees and a gushing stream. As my mother and friends were talking, I thought I would try to dip my foot along the rocky bank to see if I could feel how cold the water was. This was to no avail as the water was deep, and I thought my shoe might come off, so thought better of it.

As I approached, I heard my mother and her friends talking, so I did not notice the stinging on my foot; it was very similar to the stinging I would get in my shoulder after shoveling stalls. Then, *kaboom!* With a swift kick, off went my shoe, along with a huge snake! My mother's friends screamed, my mother screamed, and I screamed. "Did you see that!" everyone shouted. Trembling, I looked down, and sure enough, I had fang marks on top of my foot! Everyone had an opinion, but the general consensus was a copperhead or rattlesnake had bit me, and I had to run as fast as I could to the car a mile away!

While running back to the car, there were reddish streaks going up my leg, now turning black. My arch was filling with what looked like grape jelly. There was no ice anywhere so we had to go to the closest place possible which would be our little hometown hospital, about twenty miles away.

Once there, I had spiked quite a temperature, but luckily my T-strap had stopped the one fang from completely penetrating. The distance between the two fangs indicated an adult copperhead. They wanted to admit me, but my mother could take better care of me at home. I had orders to keep my leg up and on ice. Antibiotics were also ordered to take down the fever. My arch looked like something from a war zone. It would be more than weeks before I could wear shoes again. Yes, I survived once more for a reason.

The Farm

We had moved to the farm after my grandfather died. I was about eleven. My grandmother had already passed on. I remember her mostly for her cabbage soup. She was a nice enough lady though. The farm was only three miles away from town, but it may as well have been on the other side of the world.

Play days as I knew them had come to an end. Play would be baling hay and bringing the cows in at the end of the day with my "red corrective shoes." Oh how I hated those shoes. My younger sister needed them, so I was placed in them as well. One day, in the thick mud and pouring rain, one shoe was sucked into the mud as I chased home the cows. In the drenching rain, I could not find it. I was soaked and trudged home with the cows, my dog, and one shoe. I got the beating of a lifetime, as those shoes were "so expensive!"

I would often sneak food and hay to the cows. My father said we had no money, but they were starving and their rib cages were sunken in. My mother told me to stay away, but I just could not. My father had strung up electrical fencing so the cows would not wander off. At one point, he told me the fencing was off and to go get a cow. I touched it and almost landed upside down. I don't think I ever heard him laugh so hard. Such hard work for a little girl, but there was not much I could do about it.

Like a raging bull, my father would stab the cows with a pitchfork for not going in the right stalls, and I would wash off the blood with cold towels. I would sing songs to them and pet them. On one occasion, when Dad was passed out drunk on the floor, my favorite cow, ABC, had twins under a torrential rainfall. I could see she had delivered them into a water-filled pit. I tried to wake up my father, but he just groaned. I ran as fast as I could down to the barn where she had delivered the twins; however, they had drowned. When I moved them by their legs to the barn, she thought they were showing signs of life and was overjoyed! I sobbed—another alcoholic pitfall.

I admit I pleaded with God to make Dad just die. Everything would be so much better. The constant verbal abuse would end, and my mother would be free to love again. Why, God? Why?

I remember listening to the radio and hearing an ad with a jingle called "You're on the Power Line." I called in until finally someone answered, but there was not much they could do other than pray for me and my family. Why were we not like other families? I just wanted for someone to adopt me. I did my best in school and sports, and I tried to stay far away from my mother when she called the bars asking if my father was there. She was only met with, "Tell her I'll be right home soon."

In the meantime, my mother took on a part-time job to help make ends meet, which just added to my father's drinking. I knew she was not happy, but this job did get her out of the house, and she could save a bit of money for herself and us.

My father had sold the farm by then, thank God. He was working a swing shift job at a local factory. I was so relieved not to have to worry about the animals. However, he still abused the ones that were left. For the fun of it, he would drown or shoot cats and other animals. He also abused my older sister and me, constantly beating us up. At one point, I threatened to call 9-1-1, and he said, "Here, let me dial that number for you," and then he ground my face into the phone. What could I do?

This was just one of the many insults this man, whom I am not proud to even reference as my father, tortured his wife and children with. I remember a lot of the beatings, mostly with a leather belt or the strike of his hand. Sheryl got the most, as she was the most rebellious, and then I was next, because, as my father said, "Just because I can." I don't remember my younger sister being beat, but surely she watched this. She was the quiet one.

I remember one conversation I had with mom after she walked home from a town party, crying. My father was again so drunk, he had pushed a man into a swimming pool. Mom had left because she was so humiliated.

"Mom, why did you marry him?"

"I am looking into a divorce." She stared into space. Her gentle brown eyes filled with tears. I surmised she was wondering what she would do with her three girls.

I put my arm around her and said, "Let's go back to Florida, where your mother lives."

Gently the tears poured down her face. I wanted to kill him.

Not quite a year from that point in time, I was home alone with my younger sister, who was sleeping in bed. My mother and I were watching TV. I had just turned fourteen. I went to bed early, as I was so tired. I kissed Mom goodnight, and awoke to her vomiting and talking nonsensical words. I awoke my sister and told her to call the farm doctor, who lived on top of the hill from us. He told my sister to put her back to bed, but I knew something was very wrong. Again I told my sister to call him, and this time he came down.

She was taken to our small hospital, but I knew her soul and spirit were already gone from her body. When my father got home from his swing shift job, he told me I killed her because I made her watch *Medical Center*. Never would those words leave me.

She was transported to our tiny hospital and then to a larger hospital. Already feeling bad enough about what my father had said, I walked right into the ICU, with no one stopping me, looking for mom. I could not find her, so I looked under a tent, where I saw many feet moving around—another memory I will never forget.

"What are you doing to my mother?" I shouted out. They were drilling her skull with blood spewing everywhere.

A doctor spoke out, "We are trying to relieve the pressure on her brain."

They were bur holes, as I now know. I flew out, crying, and went to a park right by the hospital. No one had stopped me. No one had questioned my presence. I was living another nightmare. Now seven days after my fourteenth birthday, they were drilling my mother's head. Just great, and I had just been let into a real life *Medical Center*, so I could watch.

Had I not gone back to the hospital foyer, I would have had no ride home. I said nothing. All I knew was that I wished I'd gone with her because that, for me, was hell on earth.

Well-meaning aunts, relatives, and friends poured into the house, and through my blurred memory, I found solace in my horse that my mother had struggled to save five hundred dollars to buy for me on my thirteenth birthday. I know he was some form of angel for me. I slept in his stall and on hay bales, weeping and wondering about who was this God?

Mom's memorial service was beautiful, and I remember the concert choir, which I was a part of, coming to sing. There was only standing room, and people had spilled out onto the street.

I heard chatter all around me about why did she have to die and why was it not him? That was so surreal at my age.

Then, again she was disgraced with a flat, tiny grave marker. My father said he did not have the money for anything else. I saved money until I was able to buy two dwarf pine trees. I took care of them and planted flowers and was the only person who ever did this every year, the only daughter. I spent many days and nights there, crying.

One day, I was in for a shock. As I pulled up, the trees were gone, hacked away. My father was up to his vindictive self. He must have had a field day hacking down those special trees I had saved so hard for.

I know Mom's spirit resides within me and not in the cold block of stone marking her resting place, but taking care of her grave gave me safe harbor, oddly enough. I know my mother's presence and energy abounds everywhere. I can feel this at the strangest of times—through a smell, a thought, a look, but most of all in my heart and soul. Surely she is an angel helping others to fly when they have lost their wings.

Fracture Two

Within weeks, I heard my father talking to someone on the phone, and I just knew this was not going to be good. It sounded like they knew each other already. Surely enough, within nine months, I was told I would be at the wedding or I would have to find another place to live. She had three daughters and a son. The oldest daughter was off already off and living on her own.

My younger sister and I would not only have to share a bedroom, but also we were awoken early in the mornings to "clean the house," while her own daughters had the privilege of sleeping in.

My stepmother had to fight a hard battle to fill the shoes of my mother, and my sister and I were just reminders of her. Most of what we ate was microwaved dinners so she and my father could go out for dinner. Nothing we would do would ever be good enough in her eyes.

Of course, the public would be led to believe a whole different story. Most of my intuition came at an early age, knowing to read my father's and stepmother's moods. Quickly I could gauge the smell of alcohol, the mood in the air, and when to run and hide.

It was a true-life *Cinderella* story in the making, and it became quite apparent that I was going to be the main target. *Surely love did not live in this house anymore!*

I spent much of my time trying to avoid my stepmother. I rode my horse and kept in close touch with the local 4-H. They provided me with free trucking to horse shows and overnight camping trips. I think most of the adults who ran the 4-H knew what hell I lived in. The 4-H kept me from running with the wrong crowd. There were days, after school, when I would go for a full gallop, telling my horse everything. After all, he was my best friend. I also kept in touch with the reverend in church as well. Often I wondered if other teens my age had a life like mine—or worse. There had to be others who had it worse, and that would help me to get through my days.

My stepmother was the cream of the crop, so to speak, at parties. My younger sister and I were expected to attend these parties, especially the ones thrown during the holidays, when my step-grandparents were alive. Of course, we were threatened that we would have no place to sleep if we did not go! These parties were a major façade; game players and greedy people came to imbibe and wheel a few deals.

My mind would often drift, watching as they guzzled their drinks and lilted into an alcoholic wonderland.

However, one moment will forever be seared in my mind. A gentleman approached me and started to talk with me. He questioned me about my history as well as my future plans. He said, "You are quite smart."

I told him I wanted to be a surgeon and that the book, *The Agony and the Ecstasy* fascinated me.

He replied, "Well I think you have the brains for it!"

I quickly retorted that I did not have the money for it.

"I can put through medical school, and the only thing you would owe me is time served in our practice once you have graduated."

I was completely shocked and overwhelmed. *Wow, who is this man?* I thought.

He said, "However I do need to run this past your stepmother first."

I told him to forget it. I explained that she would never let me do this, as she had an intense dislike for me.

He retorted, "Let me try; let me try."

I watched as he found just the right moment to approach her. I saw them talking, and she almost fell over. She screamed out,

"If you would do that for her, then you would have to do that for mine," swirling and guzzling her Scotch! I had told him you cannot argue with her.

Dejected he came back to tell me that he would put up his own money; however, he knew that this would cause problems within the family, so he wished me good luck. I felt so dejected again. Her evil eyes cast that gloating, looming look of "don't even think about it."

I was sent away that summer, via my stepmother's political connections, to what she called a resort, where I slept in a shack with no lock on the door and waitressed from 6:30 a.m. until 10:00 p.m. I had no access to a car, a phone, or anything else.

Drugs and alcohol were abundant, but thankfully, I had no time for that. I was busy polishing silverware, waitressing breakfast, lunch, and dinner, and saving as much as I could for college. There was no safe place to save tips, to have privacy, or anything else. I remember one couple very well; they asked me if I would come home with them, and really thought about taking them up on it.

Fracture Three

My cousin got married at age eighteen. I had just turned seventeen. The wedding was cause for quite the party attended by relatives from near and far. Alcohol and drugs were abundant. I must say I did my share of drinking. I ended up in my cousin's bed, sick and wanting only my mother. *Oh, God, why did she have to die?*

My uncle, my mother's brother, who, in his wealthy father's eyes, could do no wrong, came up the steps to comfort me. He was in town for this celebration. This was another pathetic, surreal moment in my life.

He climbed in bed with me and took his clothes off. As I tried to push and throw him off me, he kept telling me how he could do all sorts of wonderful things for me. He could make me rich, leave his family, and all I remember was that it was the sickest thing I had ever heard of.

Music blared from downstairs, and my mind was reeling. He climbed on top of me, not to comfort me but to rape me. Others walked into the room to get high but quickly exited with pure disgust. With all my might, I threw him off and told him he was a pathetic bastard. How could he even think of such a thing! He was my mother's brother!

I left disgusted, broken, and humiliated. *Certainly*, I thought to myself, *this has to be the worst mistake of his life. What if I told anyone? What would he think when he woke up? He must have done drugs, but what kind?* I had never done any kind of drugs. *My mother must be trembling in her grave.* I tried to sleep, but I just tossed and turned.

The next morning, my father called me, saying, "Your uncle is on the phone for you."

I turned around and went out the door. He demanded I talk to him. Maybe, just maybe, he would say he was sorry—even out of his *mind*. I took the phone, trembling, and with a weak hello, he said, "Well where are you? We were supposed to meet this morning." He continued the conversation from the previous night. I could not believe it! I was speechless and just hung the phone up.

I ran up to the barn and cried and cried. *Did he not care about his wife, his children, and his own sister?* I went and hid the rest of the day so no one could find me. Later I went to sit by mother's tiny little grave stone to try to deal with this atrocity. *How could he? How dare he?*

I called my best friend, sobbing. She was the closest friend I had—more like a sister. She just listened in disbelief. "Stay away from the bastard! Your mother would be rolling in her grave if she knew about this!" I just sobbed. She just listened.

Fracture Four

My education would only reach the level of an associate degree. I could have gone to school for free with money from my mother passing, however, my father kept borrowing and borrowing against that money, stating he needed it for my stepmother.

When I got out of college, he gleefully produced loans exceeding the cost of the college had I paid in full. Thank goodness my college roommates had taken me to their homes for holidays during those two years so I could see what normal families were like.

My father lived out the rest of his life as a tortured soul. I later found out at one point, he was put in a strait jacket. He died from complications of alcoholic cardiomyopathy. His words to me were always venomous, and I dreaded being around him. He never apologized. I will always carry his words, that I killed my mother, with me. He always told me, "You are so ugly; you are a rotten motherf----n' whore; you can never do anything right around me."

Thank God for going to Adult Children of Alcoholics (ACoA) after college to know these words were never about me, but of a sick and twisted mind. My stepmother heard these words, as she listened to every call, but she never did a thing to stop it. I always wondered how anyone could listen to this type of berating and not stop it. He was in an electric type of chair for the last few years of his life, with a shotgun always at the ready in case a cat wandered by.

He left everything that belonged to my mother to my stepmother, which was most of what was left of the acreage he had not sold of the farm, including all my mother's china, silver, antiques, paintings, piano, grandfather clock, and even our childhood memories. What type of person does not at least give these personal things back?

Fracture Five

I landed a job with a new cardiologist, and I was in charge of everything. I mean everything—from the business end to the EKGs. I was so grateful, but I was also learning, and he cared deeply about language and grammar. He tore up sheets with a comma out of place. I could always tell when he'd had a fight with his wife because his ear lobe would turn red. Of course, everything is like a soap opera in a hospital, but I was able, for the most part, to get away from my alcoholic father and stepmother and survive in a very inexpensive apartment. I made friends readily. Their folks took me in like one of their own.

I met my husband during that time. He was working construction outside the hospital. He really was so nice, and that was just what I needed. Within nine months, we were engaged. He was ready to build our house! I was ecstatic. However, I knew I just had to ask questions. So we had a lengthy talk, as he was reticent to talk about this family. Yes, I have to admit, they were strange.

So what was up with that? Were there any secrets I needed to know about them—anything about him? We talked and talked. Trust and honesty were so very, very important to me.

I implored him, "I don't want to find out anything later, so please, please tell me now if there is anything I need to know."

He reassured me, time and again, "No, my family is just weird, but you are not marrying them."

Okay! We built a house, I continued to work until the birth of my first son, and then we had a daughter, and all was fairly good.

In the sixth year of our marriage, I started to note the oddest changes. My happy-go-lucky, quiet, willing man was starting to act a bit bizarre. His whole demeanor and tone took on a delusional, paranoid way of thinking. He would run and shut all the shades when he came home, telling me the FBI was watching us. His gentle mannerisms became abrasive and abrupt. I was back at work by then at the hospital, and my son was old enough to call me and tell me his daddy was hitting him. I could not believe it, but he had just started to hit me as well. I told him over and over that if he did not stop it, I would leave.

His cousin, a lawyer who was engaged to be married, had never made it to our wedding and wanted to come to visit us. I gladly said sure. While in the kitchen with Peg, I asked if she was going to have children; you know, women's chitchat.

She said she was not sure because of "the disease that ran in the family."

I said, "What disease?"

"Surely you must know, or you would not have had children."

I was in disbelief! "Um … yep, I just forgot the name. What was it again?"

"Huntington's disease."

"Oh yeah, that's it!"

"You know about Ted's father, who died in in his late forties. This would be your husband's first cousin."

"Hmm…that's right," I said, not wanting to embarrass myself. It was all I could do to hold back my tears and now my husband's odd behavior and personality swings made sense. My mind was racing.

The next morning I was on the phone with a neuroscientist from NIH. She knew how upset I was and asked me to tell her the symptoms from start to finish and drop a few names, but she could not confirm or verify.

What she could say was this. "I would bet my medical license on this, miss."

I cried out, "I want my children tested immediately! There is a fifty-fifty chance this is inherited."

"I am sorry; you have no right to know, as you may treat one child differently than the other. When they come of age, they must stand in from of a board of psychologists who will decide if they are ready or not to hear the news. Just hope a cure is found before then."

I was trembling and knew what I had to do.

I did not say a word to my husband for the next few days and tried to act normally. I continued to cook and confirm my plans to get away. One day, my husband looked at me and said, "I am going to make you live in a cage like an animal and watch you squirm."

In the meantime, I had already lined up some close friends and an apartment. I also learned as much as possible about Huntington's and the various mutations, etc. I waited for the tax check to come; it would be the only money I would have to start my life over after ten years of marriage.

Wanting this marriage annulled, I approached the family priest, and I learned he had known about this family secret all along. Outraged, I cried "How could you have known about this and never told me! I want an annulment and fast. I will not be paying any money for this either."

He just put his head down with humility. End of subject. I was infuriated, confused, and could only think about the children.

Fracture Six

The apartment signified freedom. The children were so happy to be away from the fear of being pounded against a wall and were making great friends. I put them immediately into counseling, in case there were any issues. This seemed more likely with my son. "A house is just a house," I reminded myself, "and home is where your heart is."

Not too long after, at a social club, I met a wonderful man, or at least I thought so. Cliff just blew me away with his romantic ways. He was caring, considerate, and funny. He had never married, had no children, and did not mind the fact that I did. I felt dizzy. Wow, God really was there, looking after me, or at least one of my guardian angels was. I had never been so happy—finally.

My ex kept rearing his head, and at least protection from abuse paperwork had to be filed during time, but the children were happy, and I decided to quit my job and open my own business so I could work and keep a caring eye on the two monkeys of mine. In the meantime, my second marriage seemed to be going along swimmingly. I seemed to work more hours, but oh well. We had the usual arguments that most couples get into. He had an overzealous mother, and I thanked God she did not live closer. If I said white, she said black.

I quickly became pregnant, which I thought Cliff would be thrilled about, although I was less thrilled, as I knew all that come along with pregnancy. However, he had no children, and I was eager for him to be a father. This turned out to be a disaster. I received a resounding, "No, do something about it."

I trembled and cried. "Are you sure? I thought you would be so happy!"

He asked how far along I was, and I said not too long. I went to bed crying that night.

The next day he tried to sweeten everything up. "I know of a place."

"What are you talking about?"

"Yes, just call and make the appointment."

"No, you call and make the appointment!" I cried and pleaded the whole way down. "Are you sure? What if you regret this? You have no children!"

He just stared straight ahead and never said a word. When we got there, I walked in a wrong door, but he redirected me. I pushed another door, again redirected. When the procedure was over, I could think of nothing else, but *God forgive me. Maybe this would have been a miscarriage.*

We did not speak.

Whoa! I had an aha moment as he lay in the bath and I was in bed. *How did he know how to redirect me and which doors to push?* Then it hit me. *He must have been there before. This is a nightmare.*

I went to confront him. I pulled the shower sheet away, and said, "You were there before, right?" I repeated and repeated those words, crying harder and harder.

Finally he said yes.

"You sick bastard! You sick, sick bastard."

"Wait let me explain." But by then, all I heard was white noise.

About four years into the marriage, Cliff started to become anxious and a bit distant. I asked what was wrong. He said his job was not satisfying anymore.

"Well, why don't you look for another job?"

"Oh, there is nothing out there," he said, along with every other excuse in the book.

Then one day I found a job that he qualified for. I urged him to go for the interview. "This is just up your alley with room for advancement!"

He almost did not go, but just like that, he got the job!

From then on, I thought all would be smooth sailing, and it was for a few more years, with the exception of sex.

"I'm just not a boob man. Why don't you check into having them reduced?"

I was a 36DD, so I thought maybe I should, and with a loss of self-esteem, I did.

I remember the day when I went to the plastic surgeon's office. He stated, "Most women come in to look like you. Who are you doing this for? Yourself or him?" He stated that with insurance, he would have to take off everything and I would be flat.

I said, "Well then, go ahead."

The doctor said, "Go home and think about it and come back in two weeks."

My husband was furious. By that point I had gotten used to wearing baggy tops and nothing to reveal cleavage.

Nothing I could do was right. I tried to surprise him at the office with just a coat after hours. Nothing at all would work. Then he started to travel. I could not reach him in his room at night or by cell. He would always have some excuse—no cell service or his room was moved, etc. All my friends thought he was having an affair, but there were no clues to substantiate that. What was wrong? I ironed his outfits every night, shopped for his clothes, made delicious meals, and kept the house clean.

"My partnership will be huge," he told me. "You don't need to take any social security from your paychecks. I need to put it all into buying into my partnerships, which exist in many states. I need all your money."

I was incredulous. How could this happen? Placing stats on all different pages, he showed me how we would be millionaires.

We had two computers where I worked. He was always on one at night, and of course, I was always working on one for my business. I asked him what he was doing, but he would shut the screen off in the blink of an eye if anyone got near.

In the meantime, not only was I working at up to sixty-hour workweeks, but also I managed to get my daughter her first horse, I was a 4-H leader, and I put both children through the Catholic religion. *Anything they want*, I would tell myself, *I will never be the parent my father was to me.* I threw a huge sixteenth birthday party for my daughter and had most of the prom parties and made the dinners. My son marched to the beat of a different drummer, but he was in counseling, and I tried my best to encourage him daily. Still I felt like I was a single parent, and parenting has to be the hardest job in the world.

My daughter and son were growing up so fast and getting into typical trouble for teens. Sure enough, though, salvation for my daughter was the hours spent on her horse—right down to shoveling stalls for money.

My marriage continued to falter. I had joined a nondenominational Baptist based type of church, which was wonderful, and soon Cliff started to come with me. I remember the question came up in one class, "Would you jump from side of the hill to the other if you believe in Jesus Christ?" Everyone quickly circled yes, except for my husband. This despite being raised a devout Catholic.

In the meantime there were parties and weddings we attended. At one party, he got so drunk I had to leave him there. He had piled on top of one of our friends. Even men would chide him stating, "If I had a wife that looked like yours, I would not leave her alone." We had begun to take separate cars because of actions like this. At one point, he literally pushed me around some people to get to some other men, and I was so upset I had to call my daughter to come get me.

We never danced together or held hands, and I knew what was coming, but I never imagined how surreal it was about to become.

Fracture Seven

My daughter called me from college, crying, which was weird because she is a pretty tough cookie. A computer virus had been found on campus and absolutely no one but the college techs could take it off students' devices.

When the tech addressed her computer, he found a version of disgusting porn. This took the tech aback, and he said, "Whoa, what is this?"

She said, "I never put that disgusting stuff there, and no one uses my computer!" Of course she was sick to learn from the tech that it was her stepfather who had put all this on her computer. That was when she called me to tell me about it and that she was coming home.

I told her it was late and she was upset and just to wait until tomorrow to make any big decisions. If the school counselors were available, she could go to them as well.

When I got off that phone call, everything started to congeal. Angry tears just burst out. I frantically tried to check my computer as well, but without knowing how to work around triple encryption, I knew I would have to wait until my daughter came home. I didn't sleep a wink that night.

My daughter's friend's father ran a computer shop with an FBI shield, so we took my hard drive in, and the results were brutal and appalling. I tried not to faint. Pictures, quotes, sayings, boys with boys, men with boys, words I had never heard of, things I could never imagine—but somehow, everything was starting to make some sort of sense. *He should be in jail.* That was my first and only thought. These horrific images and filth was what he was looking at, right behind me, as I worked my fingers to the bone. *Lord, help me, please.*

As I sifted through the pages and pages of filth and scum and tracked his whereabouts, I wondered if I had ever known who this man was. All of this had been triple encrypted on his computer, my work computer, and my daughter's laptop. It appeared I was just arm candy to hide his secret, deplorable lifestyle, and that was why he was never happy—he needed the façade of a marriage just to conceal the truth.

Cliff came home a few days later, and my daughter said, "Come here. I want to show you a nursing video." But it was the porn he had placed on her computer.

This stopped him dead in his tracks.

She said, "How could you?"

I came in from the dining room, and all I remember is jumping on his back and telling him to get out of the house forever! This man had come into my life with a few hundred dollars to his name, and thirteen years later, I realized he was a sociopath beyond recognition. Much later I would learn he had approached some of the boys my daughter had invited to her parties.

I don't remember who called the church that night, but the pastors came out, and my daughter and I showed them what was on that computer. They tried to calm my daughter and me, but all I could think about was if there would ever be normalcy in my life. What had I done to deserve these monsters?

The pastors decided a confrontation was to take place, as I needed an explanation. I never ever wanted to see him again, but for some insane reason, they wanted him to be accountable for what he did and explain all those love letters and cards he had written to me in the past. Of course, this was just a waste; he denied everything. They asked if he would attend a six-month course for sexual addition out west, but he said no.

"Last call for the church. Please go to our Baptist senior minister, a PhD, who puts back 99 percent of all marriages, and that will be it. We will take his word as the Bible."

Why am I even here? I thought to myself as I sat waiting for this "amazing PhD minister of theology."

Cliff will just have him believe him as well. He is so skilled at lying. Well it may as well have been Bill Clinton sitting at the chair when I sat down. His arms gently folded over the Bible, I had one hour to tell him what had happened. He just stared and did not say a word. The story unfolded from beginning to end. I said, "Remember Lacy Peterson? Remember when Scott Peterson was out searching for her body. He is just like that!"

I got up to exit, and we said a little prayer. He said after he let my ex tell his side of the story, he would be in touch. I sat in my car and cried, knowing full well he would have a field day.

The phone call came, and Dr. D said, "I would like you to schedule for an appointment."

My heart pounded, and I got ready to plead my case. However, I calmly sat down again, and we said a small prayer. Dr. D said, "Remember when you said your husband was like Scott Peterson?"

"Yes I do."

"Cliff is at least five times worse, and he is one of the worst sociopaths I have ever met! I am going to draw up a divorce contract so you do not have to get pulled into an expensive divorce attorney contract. I'll just have them write it into legalese to be signed. I will recommend he do the same. Oh, and by the way, don't just walk away from him. I suggest you run."

My heart was skipping beats. Here was one of the foremost doctors on religion and marriage telling me Cliff was one of the worst sociopaths and that I should run. Finally someone saw through this horrific façade.

I had one opportunity to confront Cliff soon after that.

"Why did you not tell me? Why? Did your mother rape you? What happened in your childhood?"

He said it started around age eight, when he raped his dog. He had also raped his sister. His mother always knew. Then he said, "If you ever tell anyone, I will deny this, deny this, deny this. I just felt you needed to know."

I think this may have been the only decent thing he ever did, as it freed me by letting me know it was never about me.

In the meantime, I went to a divorce attorney whom I thought would serve me best. I said, "Just transcribe this into legalese."

He did, but he left many loopholes to protect me to age sixty-two, or so I thought. By not filing the papers in a legally timely manner, my ex came back a year later, stating he signed under duress. However, if this had been filed properly, there would have been no way this could have happened. As a result, I have spent money beyond my means, and to this date, the case is not settled. I still have no pension, no life insurance, nothing close to what I was entitled to per the initial divorce decree had it been attached properly within six months to a qualified domestic relations order (QDRO).

Other attorneys have strongly suggested I sue the attorney for negligence and not filing within a proper time period. My ex went back to the same church to "volunteer" his time to go abroad with a pastor who is a reformed sexual addict. *What is up with that?* I thought.

During this time period, I immersed myself in counseling, but still I could not quite come to terms on how evil people can be. I truly loved this man, as I had my prior husband. Here I had been married a total of twenty-three years! I had such a capacity for love but had fallen into a deep depression.

Then I had to deal with a lot of unsolicited advice from people telling me to just snap out of it and move on. This is when I realized depression is real. One does not just "snap out of it." This is truly a trying form of losing oneself and one's voice. *How could something like this happen to someone like me?*

Next came time to pull out a mask and then go home to wrap up in a blanket. There were times when I prayed I had enough food in the pantry so I did not have to leave the house. Profound darkness wrapped its veil around me once again.

Unless you have ever walked this walk, please do not even attempt to understand it. I was one of those who never could understand battle. "Never judge anyone" is a motto I truly try to live by now. People living in the nicest houses with the greatest marriages and the most money have lost their battles to depression. The hardest battle is talking about it. The hardest part of the battle is losing family on account of sheer ignorance.

Fracture Eight

Aunt Jen was my godmother who lived a little more than two hours away from me. She had married the love of her life, Bill, who died early on. She never remarried. I honestly cannot describe the agony of what she went through, but surely it must have been similar to losing your right arm.

She continued to check in on my sisters and me from time to time. She had a deep love of horses, which was mutual. She also owned a small piece of property on top of the hill.

She was a tough bird, but I could tell, when I looked deep into her eyes, that she understood pain. She also understood when she was not welcome, but she came up every Christmas Eve to share her quirky gifts with all of us. There was an underlying current of bad blood between brother and sister. She adored my father, and I will never know why, as she was a victim to his tyrannical rages. She was a smoker, which he abhorred.

Interestingly enough, in listening to my relatives speak, I learned that my grandfather, whose death had been ruled a farm accident after a farm tractor tipped over on him, was not really so. It was believed my father wanted the farm in his name so badly that his greed caused him to rig a tire too big for the tractor that day, which the relatives could prove. Thus the tractor rolled over, causing my grandfather's demise.

There was quite a bit to learn about Aunt Jen, so when she spoke, I listened. Years later, she asked if I would accompany her to a well-known hospital, a place she had already been to regarding a diagnosis. It was there she told me she had lung cancer and had it for more than a year. This did not come as a surprise to me, but I begged her to quit. She emphatically stated *no*.

I knew this doctor she was seeing, and I asked him, "What would you do if this was your mother?"

"This is a hard one to be sure. However, this is a choice only you and your aunt can make. There is chemo and radiation. But, I would tell my mother to go on playing golf and doing the things she enjoys."

When I looked at her, I knew her mind was already made up. We hugged, and I said, "Let's go to McDonald's for a vanilla cone." Oh, how she loved those cones.

The only requirement made of me was that I not tell a soul. That was very hard. However, I made the promise and kept it for more than a year, and we stayed in close contact. Only her best friend, who lived near her, knew. We stayed in close contact by phone, and she assured me everything was fine. Oh, that damned word, *fine*.

Early one morning, I received a phone call. "Can you come down right away?"

"Who is this?"

"This is Jen's best friend, June, and I cannot get through to her. She is wasting away."

"Did she not tell you about the lung cancer and how far it has spread?"

"What? No, she has not told me anything, and I have not seen her at all! I think you may be the only person that can help," June said. "Please come down."

My daughter happened to be off from nursing school, and we headed down.

On arrival, Jen's door was unlocked, and we could hear shuffling in her bedroom. We sat calmly on the couch, and when she appeared, I saw a ghost of a woman. Her pride and vanity had been stripped away. She turned toward the wall and told us to leave. Instead, I wrapped my arms around her and hugged her gently. I knew we needed to do something now.

The bathroom was filled with soiled clothes, and she had been trying to wash them out in the tub. Calls were made to many a doctor and to hospice. She needed to be hospitalized, which she was, but then she was quickly released. I argued with the doctors that she was at risk of falling. It was insane. I got her new clothes and slippers, and we talked. She assured me she had a lawyer and will. She wanted her Catholic priest to give last rites. I listened but also tried to reassure her.

"Can I call loved ones now? Please?" I begged

A resounding *no* was what I received. I felt so helpless. This is what hospice calls death with dignity—respecting the patient's one last wish. For Aunt Jen, that would come as no one knowing her battle. However, that would leave my hands tied and a lot of friends and family not understanding what I needed to do out of respect and compassion. I knew her demise was not far away.

Finally hospice stepped in after she did fall when I was not there. Again I received a call to hurry and come down. After a few days, they said she was holding on for something, and it could possibly be she was sensing my presence. They asked if I would lie in bed with her and "let her go." This lasted a little over a half hour. Hospice had been listening in, and they said they had never heard anything like that. I waved them on to go back to my hotel room.

The nurses said, "We will be calling you before you even get there."

Sure enough the phone rang. Aunt Jen had passed on to our eternal Father.

Then came the barrage of phone calls to friends and family who did not even know she had been sick. This was followed by explanations, reasoning's, and the ignorance of others. Many of these people still hold grudges and do not speak to me to this day. They had no idea that I was involved in her care for almost two years and of my struggle to uphold and honor her last wish.

Because many of our relatives were not named in Jen's will, they think I pushed my beloved aunt down the steps. I have come to realize you cannot control what other people think. It just is what it is. The lesson I learned from this is that there are always two sides to a story, and I must never rely on one person's side of the story. There may be invaluable knowledge in a side I have not yet heard about.

Aunt Jen had chosen to leave money, which was quite a shock as no one thought she had anything, to six heirs, including me. Since I was left the most, I gave her a proper burial service, at her favorite country club, and made sure everyone was notified.

I took a portion of my money and took the six heirs and their kin to Aunt Jen's favorite island, Aruba. This would be dubbed Aunt Jen's Aruba trip.

She is buried next to the love of her life.

Fracture Nine

I ended up selling that house of nightmares that I had shared with Cliff. I could not bear to live in the house where Cliff had lived such a deviant sociopathic lifestyle right under my nose. By selling the house, and with my aunt's proceeds, I had enough to afford a townhome about fifteen miles away from where I had raised my children.

That is where Steve had come into my life. He was a nice man and just what I needed on all accounts, although this would be a long distance relationship. We had something that most people do not find in a lifetime, yet something on my end was not compassionate to his needs. This man had survived a brutal bout with cancer so he was not self-critical, and was secure in who he was. We shared our stories and what we hoped our future would become. Yes, he very well was the one for me, but with so much going on in my life there was a lot of family disorder in his which I was not ready for. Little did I know he would become a crucial thread later in my life for healing.

My daughter was finishing her nursing degree and finding her place in life. My son was done with his army stint, and I had provided him yet another used car and enough money to get a degree in information technology. He already had one marriage under his belt that he had never told me about, and he continued to march to his own drummer. He was sent for training with a *Fortune* 500 company in Las Vegas, which was going to change a lot of lives forever.

The phone call came in about seven in the morning. "Mom, Josh has been in a terrible accident in Las Vegas! The police called me, and we have to go out immediately because he is not expected to live!"

"What!" I cried out. I wanted all the details, but she didn't have many, so I called the hospital and made immediate travel arrangements.

I remember everyone on the plane to Vegas being happy, happy people. I was sitting there in disbelief. Could this really be happening? Luckily Steve whom I was dating at that time helped me out with the arrangements and place to stay and such. I don't know what I would have done without his help and the help of my friends.

Upon arrival we were escorted to the highest of three levels of the ICU. I had worked in a hospital, but what I saw shocked me. Josh was barely alive, intubated, and hooked up to every lifesaving apparatus available. Almost every bone had broken. His heart rhythm was not in sync, and he was coding. He also had two brain hematomas. The neuroscience doctor said it would probably be best if he did not survive, as he would probably have the mental capacity of a two- or three-year-old.

The police were there, and I was trying to piece together what had happened Apparently Josh had fallen asleep at the wheel due to the heat, and he'd crossed the meridian lines and struck another driver head-on. Although it is purported that this driver was saturated with coke, another life was taken that day. So if Josh survived, he would be looking at manslaughter charges.

Dear Lord, I prayed, *This is just too much for me! Please help my son and me.* I wept and do not remember much about the next few days. They were a blur with Josh battling for his life and me filling out paperwork for next of kin. I was deluged with phone calls, but the cop had befriended me, thank God.

Then, *bang!* A woman appeared in the room, telling me she would take over from here on.

I said, "What are you talking about?" And then I asked social services to escort her out of the room immediately. *Just what I need*, I thought, *someone playing a joke on me.*

She said, "I am his wife; Josh flew me down two weeks ago. We were married in one of the chapels, and by the way, I am three months pregnant."

I stared at my daughter in disbelief and then back at her. "You really need to leave immediately. My son never mentioned any of this to me, and he is barely alive."

The cop looked at me and said, "Look, I will go check this out." Social services took the woman out of the room. I thought this had to be the worst joke in the world.

Looking into the cop's eye when he returned, I could tell the story was true. He said he had watched the tape, and I was incredulous! Josh had done it again; married without telling anyone, not even his own mother or sister. Somewhere deep inside, I knew I had to welcome a stranger into my life, carrying what would be my grandchild, and have her takeover my son's paperwork and make his health decisions. Things were shaky at best.

"The main thing is that we focus on Josh and his health now," I clearly stated. She agreed and was quiet. She told me she had to go home, as she had another daughter from a different marriage to tend to. Also my daughter had to go back to college.

So with the demise of my business, I did what any mother would do. I dug into the savings I had and stayed until Josh gradually showed signs of improvement, defying all odds.

Slowly, Josh was moved down in trauma units and had multiple surgeries. Then he was sent to a rehab facility. I had spent way more than I thought I was going to. The cop had already placed an ankle bracelet on him, as he was looking at manslaughter charges.

One day in the rehab facility, he looked outside at the people and said, "I don't understand why I cannot go out there. It's not like I killed anyone."

That was when I took the newspaper clipping out of my purse and showed it to him. He read it in disgust, threw it, and gently cried. Of course, he had no memory. He did not remember his wife either. He had no idea of any marriage or baby on the way.

Finally he was able to stand trial. With the loving help of a girlfriend of mine who had moved to Las Vegas and who was able to post bond for him, he was able to return to Arkansas and settle for a bit before returning for his big trial. The cop recommended the least penalty possible to the judge. However, he told me he was not in control of what the judge would do.

The sentence was community service, an ankle bracelet, and restitution. A very unhappy family on the other side had to be dismissed separately because there was so much tension and shouting. Hoping beyond hope, I thought surely Josh would see the reason why God spared his life and that there was a reason he was still alive. He had much more work here to do.

He was the father of a beautiful baby girl, and I was a grandmother! Distance made it hard for me to see her, and the marriage was already rocky. I had a feeling it was not going to solidify. Another innocent baby trapped in what I felt would soon be a divorce, but I guessed she was here for a reason. She was so beautiful!

The time came when I flew with my daughter to Arkansas to see my granddaughter baptized. *Moments like this are priceless. You cannot buy memories*, I kept thinking. I became a bit closer with Beth, his wife, and Arie, his stepdaughter. All in all it was a fairly good trip. But my son did not seem very humble regarding the accident, nor was he wearing his ankle bracelet.

Beth told me of trips he'd made to the park, which he could not remember. Basically they were trips in which he became inebriated, drinking a bottle of vodka, and have everything, including his wallet, stolen. He related these stories to me, but he had no memory at all when he woke up, and he would wake up in the strangest places. He always had an excuse. Most of these excuses had to deal with PTSD.

I was on overload as he complained about his job, his wife, and his lack of money. Quickly I would retort how lucky he was to be alive and have these issues to complain about, but he never wanted to hear this. It was always about him. Josh has never thanked me for staying with him all that time out in Las Vegas or anything else. He has never sent me a birthday card or a Mother's Day card.

Huntington's disease has is caused by an autosomal dominant mutation and if one parent is affected there is a 50% chance the child will be affected. There is genetic testing now possible, however, to my knowledge one still needs to be of a competent age and hold up to psychiatric evaluation to hear the possibility of these devastating results. Schizophrenia and mental disorders are hallmark features of this disease. Movement disorders may or may not occur and every case is judged to be different and on a case by case basis.

In hope that his daughter would be his saving grace, I saved for all of them to come to Atlantic City, along with my daughter, to see the ocean. There we had a family portrait taken. This was the last family portrait before the demise of his marriage to Beth. He constantly complained about what a horrible wife she was and that he never should have married her.

"Josh work things out for the sake of your daughter," I said. "Get a shared custody agreement."

All I heard was excuses and how he wanted full custody. There were many times I could hear it in his voice that he had been drinking. He had also been taking up with my older sister, who had never had children and knew nothing of being a parent. She was the know-it-all type. She also had money.

Josh had taken up with yet another gal named Lisa who had three children of her own. This was quite the arrangement. Now, when he had custody of his daughter, she had instant playmates, a dog, and I was finally getting calls. Lisa never really talked to me; she was quite shy.

One night, Josh went out with some friends, and there was a fight at a bar. The police checked everyone's licenses, and just like that, Josh was back in jail! I could not believe it! He was tagged as a fugitive from justice from Las Vegas. He was in jeopardy of losing the one thing he had going for him—his job. Lisa battled for him, and five or six days later, she got him out of jail.

Some years ago, Josh stopped paying restitution to the family of the man he had killed. Now he was going to be sent back to court in Las Vegas again! Josh was begging for money, but I had none to offer, and no one else did either. They were sick of his antics, except his aunt, who unbeknownst to me, gave him the money.

Lisa and Josh flew out to Vegas, where he faced criminal charges. While there, he had his pay check attached and used my sister's money to take a nice vacation and marry Lisa. He told no one. Again! This was the third marriage about which he told no one.

With my granddaughter now turning five, I just had a craving to see her again. I was struggling because I knew she was forgetting my face, even though she knew my familiar voice on the phone. I thought about it long and hard and found the deal of a lifetime.

I called my son and said, "I want to see my granddaughter. She has been through so much! If I put this trip I found on a credit card, would you be able to swing it by coming to Florida with my little munchkin?"

He thought about it and asked his manager. "Sure, Mom, no problem. That would be great!"

"Are you sure? I cannot get my money back." He assured me over and over that it would be fine.

I felt I should call Beth just to be sure Josh had told her. She said he had mentioned something and that would be okay with her. I was ecstatically happy!

The trip was approaching, and Beth called to see if I knew what was going on. I replied, "No what?"

"Josh is in jail." My heart sunk! "Is this some type of joke? He is supposed to be coming down here in a few days!"

"I know, but he has just been jailed for domestic violence against Lisa"

"You have got to be kidding me. Tell me everything please."

She went on with the story as much as she knew. I could not believe it; I always told him he was never to hit anyone, especially a woman. I asked her if she would be able to come down, but she could not. "How about Arie, my granddaughter's half-sister? She is a mature twelve-year-old and probably would love to come." And with that, I began to call the airline and the hotel, and I rearranged the trip.

My son called me, stating again he had been the victim.

I said, "How could you? I don't want to hear it. Get yourself tested for Huntington's and get help. You have VA benefits; use them."

My daughter is another story. She has had everything in life. Her horse, trips everywhere, clothes, etc. But I had also flown my daughter down three times, once with six of her girlfriends. They ended up trashing my place. I drove them to Disney, rented a huge condo, and no one ever said thank you. My daughter has had a DUI, and when I had to come back up for a doctor's appointment, her venomous tongue lashed out at me so harshly that I was left crying in the driveway. If I'd had more money, I would have called a cab and gone somewhere else.

Yes, there was alcohol in the house again. This was evidenced by the fact that she was late with a car loan payment I'd signed on, and several times last year, I had to give her the money to pay it—all this despite having a fantastic job as a nurse. I recognized many familiar signs with her as well. She was quick with the tongue and denied having said things she did say. She became cold and calculating with me.

The hardest thing I have ever done in my life was to disengage myself from my daughter. I called her at least twice weekly, only to be greeted with a cold response. I saw her on Facebook, but she would not answer a message. Simply put, I know, and my friends do too, that I was the best mother I could have been.

Could it be that both children were affected by the Huntington's gene, or was one affected and the other alcoholic? Whatever the case, I was left heartbroken, simply heartbroken. However, if Huntington's is at fault, then once again, another life has been afflicted, and by all means, we need more research to stop the disease.

More importantly, we need to stop this gene from being passed on from generation to generation through further testing before becoming parents. For further research on this, google Huntington's disease; it comes in many different mutations and at multiple ages.

Fracture Ten

Ann was a wonderful, deeply spiritual Christian counselor. My family was dysfunctional mainly because of my mother's untimely death. My two sisters and I reacted differently. One became an alcoholic and dependent on drugs. The other built walls so thick, they were impenetrable. However, I had such such good friends I could rely on and confide in. A few were just like sisters to me, and they always will be, and for them I will be forever grateful.

After many years of counseling Ann finally said, "You are free, and you have always wanted to move to Florida. Go, spread your wings, help others, and get out of this cold, gloom, and doom. I can see you there. You have some family there, and it could be a new start for you. You have healed from what would have put most women in the hospital, and much more."

The more I thought about Ann's advice, and with my adult children out of the house, this seemed like a true possibility. But this also meant having to see my uncle again. Then there were my three cousins and my aunt. I worried that their children and grandchildren may have been a victim of his sexual antics. Did they already know about his advances toward me? Nothing I did was good enough though for them. Maybe they did, and I was a painful, unwanted reminder?

However, I was hopeful my sister and I could reestablish a long lost friendship and that I could play a role in my beautiful niece's life.

Unfortunately none of that happened. Money played a significant role in my sister's life. She seemed to define herself and others by the almighty dollar. Could that be because of how poor we were when we grew up? If you had it great, but if you did, not watch out. I went to great lengths to point out how short life is and that there is no room for holding grudges. Sadly she did not agree.

Florida sure is big, I thought. Was it true that there was sunshine every day there? *Hmm ... maybe Florida is where I belong. Maybe my heavenly mother and God are trying to tell me something. Baby steps*, I thought. Baby steps.

Fracture Eleven

My cousin helped me moved in. My relatives were busy with their own lives and their own ways of doing things. I guess I had hoped to blend in more, and I missed my friends deeply from back home. Had I made the wrong decision? Coming from a small town to a city of more than one million was quite the challenge. I was thrilled to be able to see more of my very talented niece, but my sister was cold and impartial. She only visited me once, and that was because I had a seizure while I was with her at her daughter's play. I have always tried to blend in with everyone, high, low, and in between.

I believe that, to avoid pain and hurt, people wear many masks and try to hide behind walls they've built over time. Masking pain comes in many forms, from autoimmune disease to diseases and deep-down anger and depression. Some people are just reminders of the past; they stir up unwelcome memories.

We are all the same in energy and spirit. No matter how much we see in a smiling face and in a person's demeanor, we must remember that all of us are fighting some type of battle. Truly, I take more time out now to say "please" and "thank you." In some ways, I feel we are becoming human drones.

With technology in place, we are reticent to make a phone call or make a trip and give that desperately needed hug. Yet, we are extremely quick to judge others. This is something we are all guilty of.

In the meantime, Ms. Directionless (this is what I called myself then) tried to find herself in this huge area, and I am just thankful for my GPS. In my second year in Florida, I was empowered to become a life coach and started up a new business. I have always had a passion for helping others, especially walking the walk of others who have been in my shoes. I had hoped the business would take off quickly; however, in the land of the snowbirds, vacationers, and the jobless there is really not a lot of demand for life coaches. Alternatively, in California, the employment rate was high for life coaches. My CEO gave it to me straight, and said, "Just move." My inner voice said, "Wow, I just got here."

Fracture Twelve

Last year, I met a man outside the movies with his brother. Oh was he full of himself, yet there was something endearing about him, so we wound up dating. It was not too long before we knew "this was it". We would say a short prayer before eating, but he was not without piss and vinegar. I became his sounding board to listen to when his business was bad, and before long, he was talking possible marriage. However I was finally fishing, collecting shells, and letting the sunset dance its brilliant radiance around me, soothing my heart for once. Time waits for no one, however.

Tom started to complain of shoulder pain.

"Wow that area is where your rotator cuff, and you will probably need a steroid shot." Tom received many, many steroid shots, but I said "Tom, that is just not right, unless you are not getting the real steroid shots."

He had all kinds of offers from practitioners, ranging from cutting the nerves in his spinal column to chiropractic manipulations and taking herbs for the pain. Confusion set in, and I pondered how different medicine was practiced in different states.

In the meantime, we had so much fun. My daughter met him, as did a few distant relatives. He was so full of life, always throwing a punch line or two. Tom had a great love of family and really got what life was all about, and that was what I fell in love with.

I researched doctors and got him to one I was certain had gone to a great medical school. There he had an MRI. He called with bad news. There was a huge tumor on his thoracic spine (aka T-spine). Another MRI of his brain showed the cancer had spread all over.

Holding hands, we sung "Ave Maria" at sunset on his favorite beach and island. He died a few weeks before his fifty-second birthday. He left behind a beautiful daughter and many good friends.

Good-bye Tom, you certainly touched a lot of lives.

Fracture Thirteen

The fracture I don't ever want to talk about, but I will, touches the basic, raw nerves of life. Because I had moved to Florida, I begged my ex to take my son to obtain his driver's license, but he could not be pulled away from the pool boy. This was also after my first seizure, which I thought had been stress induced, when a tiny, concerning area was found in my brain. This was thought to have been a small stroke.

I had worked for a group of neurologists and knew the implications. In the years that followed, I was placed on medications and joined support groups and became a mentor to others with similar diagnoses. Just like others, I was in denial, thinking, *This will never ever happen again.* I knew I needed to eliminate much of the stress in my life.

Of course, I had repeated MRIs on the off chance this was not the correct diagnosis. After moving to Florida, I went for an MRI from a highly recommended neuroradiologist. I was not given my results for more than a week, something I could not understand.

Why in the world did I have to wait that long? I found Florida to be really different when it came to healthcare, to say the least.

Finally, I went to the neurologist's office. "I have a right to my records. Please let me see them now."

He handed them to me very hesitantly with his head down. Now, I am well versed in the medical field, and I read in my file, "glioma most likely diagnosis." Of course, that was a slow growing brain tumor!

"You have got to be kidding me. Now I know why you would not let me get the results or read them to me over the phone. Unbelievable!"

"Well, maybe that is not true," the doctor remarked.

I said, "You sent me to him; you said he was the best and would have no other radiologist read the report!" I deserved to know this information right away, not ten days later during an appointment.

Then, of course, the studying began. The symptoms I was having were consistent. This was a nightmare. What would I do? I had no real family to turn to, except my friends, who were awesome.

I went back to the neurologist who had my records back home. He set me up with a neurosurgeon and neuroradiologist. Each had varying opinions, but all were in agreement that the area was too close to the brain stem, which could not be biopsied; it was just too dangerous, even in this day and age. The best we could do was an MRI in another year to check for growth.

My family doctor was great and very understanding. "You really need to get your family on board immediately."

I just looked at her thinking, *If only you knew.* My health insurance premium was though the roof, and the cost of medicine was way too prohibitive. People may have judged me by my looks, but an invaluable lesson was repeated for me that day. Never judge people by what they look like because you never know what type of battle they may be up against.

Now this was not the type of thing I wanted to go around announcing, so when I reached out to my daughter, an RN, I was met with "why don't you have your friends help you?" I have been demeaned and screamed at by her, and frankly, I empowered myself to reclaim my self-esteem and my voice when I was diagnosed. I just decided that she must have had her own battles to fight.

Once again my friends helped me through these trying times. Depression came raging back into my life. This was supposed to be the best time of my life; I had gone through so much, learned so many lessons, made the big move, and was starting to feel empowered again. I joined a group of wonderful women at church, who were there for me when I needed them.

Certainly I had made great strides in believing that I could deal with whatever comes my way. I felt then, as I do now, that I have a lot of "work" left to do here on earth.

However, if anyone you know has had a seizure for any reason—stress, meningitis, lack of oxygen, PTSD, brain trauma, etc.—please be the voice for greater research and exploration.

Fracture Fourteen

"Move back," my friends told me. "You have so much to offer, and Florida is just so big."

It is true that making friends in midlife is hard; many people are married or already have their group of friends. However, as my friend always said, if I could not make friends, then no one could. So I acclimated to the beautiful weather and now cherish my friends, old and new, who are like family to me.

Few visitors have come, and there is nothing worse than loneliness and isolation. However, this summer a friend of mine from back home asked if she could visit. Having just broken up from a lengthy, rocky relationship, she was ready to party! I live close to the beach, but I don't go all that much. I don't know why. However, she was ready to party *large and in charge*. I could not do all that much because of discs I ruptured in a car accident and medicine that made me tired.

However, we did manage to make it out and about. One day, she wanted to the beach right down the road from me.

"I really don't go there much, but let's go walking and check out guys." I sighed as we started down to the beach.

Not more than a few hundred feet into our walk, we saw two men holding a sign: *Free beer for hugs.* She took off a running, and I followed up. I did not want to drink, for sure, but we sat down and started talking to Vance and Vance (that's not a mistake). They seemed nice enough and were down from the north on vacation. It was interesting—they lived less than six hours away from where I used to live.

We ended up having a conversation with them, and they were very funny. One had a condo down here and used it part-time. They joked about their names and occupations. I am not much for the sun; I am fair skinned and did not want to be out too long in the sun's strong rays. We also had a lot to see and do, but promised we would meet up with them the next day—same time, same place. "There is something about those two," I said to my friend, and she laughed. Little did I know how unbelievable life was about to become for me.

The last day they were here, we were getting lunch at a tiki hut across from the beach.

"My name is not Vance. It is Shane. And I am not a cook in the Air Force. I am an Air Force flight fighter!"

"Yeah, right," I said.

He held a card up high and said, "Here this will prove it."

"Yeah, right," I said again. "You guys have done nothing but just blow yourselves up since you have been here."

"Oh you don't believe me; you don't believe me!"

At that time, Vance let his guard down, and I pulled the card away. I almost fell off my chair! Of the billions of people in this world, there it was: Vance with Cliff's last name, which is not common! I stared in disbelief!

Vance said, "What's the matter? What's the matter!"

"I do not get it."

"What, you don't like my name or somethin'? Wait, I had a cousin who moved out your way. Couldn't be something to do with him, could it?"

This was an out of body moment for me! I got even quieter.

He then yelled out, "What did you know him? Did you? You could not have f----d him, could you? The whole family knows he's gay!"

I just said, "I have to go to the bathroom, excuse me."

"Well, you are going to tell me if you know him—or what is going on—when you get back!"

In the bathroom, I had to wipe down my face. *What to do?* My mind was spinning out of control. *How could this happen? This has to be divine intervention. Here we go again, proof of this psychotic sociopath. I just cannot face this guy or deal with this. I have healed from my past and cannot face this part of my life again. I guess I will just run home.*

My head pounded. *Help me, dear Lord!*

I came out of the bathroom, and there stood Vance, tapping his foot and demanding to be told what was going on. I was still speechless. I just threw my insurance card at him.

"Crap! Shit!" He was completely dumbfounded. He looked at me. "How could you be so dumb? Everyone knew."

What the hell! Off we both went with the promise to talk later.

Yes, and later we met to discuss how a beautiful woman (of heart and soul) like me gets one pulled over on her like that. I then learned all the details about Cliff's move across the state from west to east, what the relatives thought, and what everyone knew. How could I be so duped?

Then again, what had God been trying to tell me out on that tiny beach with all those millions and millions of people? Maybe it was time for justice to be served after all. Worst of all, Cliff had remarried and was pulling the same stunt on another woman. This, to me, is when gay is just so, so wrong. A deviant, sociopathic man, whom I thought I had finally put out of my mind, flooded back via his first cousin on a tiny little beach.

I searched for answers and prayed in silence. *Lord, is this why I moved to Florida? To find solace, completion, and a reaffirmation of what I already knew from his cousin?* Was this vindication? A catharsis?

I knew the Lord did not make mistakes. Might I have been in training for something much bigger than I could possibly know?

My mind jumped back to a woman I had seen a little over a year ago while a band was getting ready to set up. She was drinking a Coke and was accompanied by another lady who was drinking water. There were about twenty people waiting to hear this band. I do not know what made me go out that night, other than I was feeling alone and heard there was a good band.

The woman turned around and touched me and said, "God has spoken and told me to tell you that you have been chosen and will help thousands and thousands of people." She also stated that it seemed I would help people in the distance, which I took to mean in the future. Bewildered, I stared at her in disbelief and at her friend. She was drinking a soda. When she went to the bathroom, I asked her friend, "Is she normal?"

Her friend looked at me and said, "I have been friends with her for twenty years, and this rarely happens; sometimes once a year, sometimes none. If she tells you this, then you can rest assured she speaks the truth. She does not drink, and you should feel honored, as I have seen these miracles come true."

I got off the bench and went home in disbelief. I thought, *how can I help that many people?*

Truly I listen a lot more to God now. Also I was invited by a friend to go to another church, where the pastor held class inside her home. When we met for the first time, she came to me and said, "You are going to help many many people to come in the future. I cannot tell when but it will come soon.

I am not afraid or scared anymore. I have a calling of mind, body, and soul. I have witnessed much in my life. God uses people all the time as conduits if they just listen deeply enough. Through my depression and times of isolation, I wish I had listened more to God and had not caved to the fears and worries of this life. But I did not.

Miracles happen all the time, and if we just listen and look for them they are abundant! The peace I feel now does not stop me from all worry, fear, and stress, but now I know who is in control and that I never did have control. All of these fractures were teaching me how I may help someone else someday.

Worry and fear will eat you alive, just like the fractures in my life nearly consumed me. Surely these were not placed upon me for fun. However, I am not here to judge people or to bear witness to what is morally right and wrong. God has that covered.

We are lost characters, making our own plans, devising our own wisdom, and travelling our own paths. What is your great commission in life? How can you touch someone you know is hurting or who has lost their way?

We must go forth and remind ourselves that we are nothing without our faith and love, which will evolve into peace, justice and freedom.

Clearly it has taken me a long time to learn how to free oneself and empower with forgiveness. I ran across a saying once that empowered me to tape it to the refrigerator. It is now turning shades of yellow. In times of chaos, I go back and read and reread this.

I am making a choice to forgive you. By doing so, I free myself from the bond I had with you through hatred, anger, resentment, or fear. I take back my power and gain the freedom that only forgiveness can bring. You cannot hurt me and cannot control me. I forgive for myself.

How *awesome* is that? Surely women of all ages need to find their inner voices. These voices reside in all of us, yet most of us have our inner voices on mute. We are too afraid to use our voices and turn inward to face demons such as depression, loss of self-esteem, drug and alcohol addiction, self-abuse, and the list goes on and on.

Recently, while I was at a mall, in the front of a window at a very popular lingerie store, I stopped to admire a beautiful outfit on a mannequin. There was a young lady next to me looking at the same outfit. I turned toward her and noticed tears running down her face. I thought for a moment, and realized my inner voice must address this.

Quietly, I said, "She is wearing a beautiful outfit, and I wish I could afford that. Do you wish you could own that outfit?"

She put her head down and said, "No, I could never have that outfit. I am so fat! My legs don't look like that. My face does not look like that."

She was despondent, so I thought about this and said, "No you do not look like that mannequin, or the picture from the page she is featured on. She is completely airbrushed. Her legs, arms, face, and stomach are all airbrushed!"

She stopped for a moment and looked at me. "What do you mean by that?"

I went on to explain the methods fashion magazines and retailers use to make models look more like mannequins and less like real people.

Her eyes brightened a bit, and as I went to introduce myself and shake her hand, I could tell she had been cutting herself.

"Ahh ... bet you have been not eating right either? Throwing up Mom's meals, I bet, right?"

Her head went down again, and she indicated she had been.

"Hey, let's sit down over here a bit and just talk for a minute. I am not here to judge you, but let's just hang out for a minute. I know how bad life can get."

"Well, okay but just for a minute."

I told her a bit about my life in high school and how hard it was. But most of all, I talked about how great she was!

I taught her some mirroring techniques she could use to remind herself that she is wonderful every day for the rest of her life. She made a vow to go home and paste a few of these affirmations to her mirror and to never ever cut herself again. She promised also to eat normally; she was stick thin.

I reminded her to never let anyone or anything define her identity for her. I told her this was going to be lifelong battle, but after a while, she would recognize all the signs. Reminding herself of how amazing she was would become easier every day, and she would reflect confidence and exude radiance.

"You know," she said smiling, "my father has been telling me the same things, but it just never hit me like this!"

"Sometimes you just have to see it from a different point of view and hear it from someone not in your family. By the way, what does your father do anyway?"

"Oh, he is a psychiatrist. I am so happy to have met you!" she exclaimed.

A few hours later, we parted ways, but never was I so happy to have helped a person find her inner voice. Many of us don't realize we have one. We spend our lives being so busy that we cannot wait to sleep. Then we tell everyone else how busy we are so we don't have time to address these problems. On the other end, we become depressed and dread leaving our houses. We become mired in addiction and stuck behind a wall or a mask.

You cannot go wrong if you use your inner voice, no matter what has happened in your life. If you have been a victim, use your voice to empower other victims. Join a group, a club, write a journal—do not remain silent.

Silence takes away your power. If this happened when you were young, your power was taken away without your permission. Now is the time to make a huge contribution to others and yourself—reclaim your voice!

You never know what others are facing, and believe it or not, it may be exactly what you have gone through! We are not just faces passing without words, thoughts, and deeds connecting us.

The process of reclaiming our inner voice includes letting go of the past, and making peace with what you can. This is the hardest challenge you may face to stand up for yourself. Some people may resist but that is okay, just do it for yourself.

Recently I contacted Steve, my long distance love. It has been over seven years, but I felt there were unfinished words that I needed to apologize for. You see I was still writhing from the abuse and pain from my second marriage that I thought I had gotten over. Calmly he listened to what I felt went wrong in the relationship, and we both agreed we could have done things better. He has been married for four years, and deeply in love. They have no secrets. I congratulated him, as tears of joy ran down my eyes. He deserved no less, and I felt a tremendous relief.

I have reached out to family members without the same result, but just knowing that I tried has made me the better person and does not define me. Know that it is not about you. The fractures that have happened to me in my life, and many more, that are not in this book, are constant reminders that many people have it worse and many better. There is a difference between forgiving and forgetting. Heinous acts are yours to choose to forgive or forget. Somehow, I cannot forget these heinous acts, but I can choose to help other women find their voice. We all have a story. Stories can make or break us, so let us begin by sharing our stories.

Conclusion

Although this book represents my story and thoughts, many details have been left out. Please know that you will never be able to thrive or have purpose in life until you address what has happened in your life. I beg of you, no matter how hard this will be (and it will be), find a coach or counselor and let your voice be heard. Nothing is so terrible that it cannot be heard.

The universe is listening, trust me; it is waiting for your voice and the collective voices of others. Only then can we make a difference. Only then can we change each other, hug one another, and know that no matter how many scars, wounds, or fracture lines we face, it was never ever about us!

Be benevolent.
Be brilliant.
Be brave.
And know *you* are never alone.

If I were to remain silent I would be guilty of complicity.

—Albert Einstein

Journal Page

Journal Page

Journal Page

Journal Page